COLLABORATIVE DEBATING

Tale Publishing

First Published 2016

Copyright © 2017 Margaret Hepworth All rights reserved.

ISBN-13: 9780994439970 (Paperback)

ISBN-10: 0994439970

National Library of Australia Cataloguing-in-Publication entry:

Creator: Hepworth, Margaret, author.

Title: Collaborative Debating / Margaret Hepworth.

Target Audience: For adolescent children.

Subjects: Debates and debating--Study and teaching (Secondary)

Debates and debating--Textbooks.

Public speaking--Textbooks.

Tale Publishing

Melbourne Victoria

Contents

About the Author: Margaret Hepworth | The Gandhi Experiment.............1
The Gandhi Experiment - the freshest ideas in mindful education! 2
Why Collaborative Debating? 4
Educational Theory and Practices Underpinning Collaborative Debating ...6
Two Important Methodologies 8
Key Learnings and Outcomes of Collaborative Debating......................... 11
Collaborative Debating Begins 13
Collaborative Debating - The Process 15
The Mentor's Guidances 19
Teaching the Role of Mentor to your Students 23
Suggested Topics for Debates 24
Conclusion 25
Other Uses of the Collaborative Debating Technique 26
COMING SOON: The NEW Gandhi Experiment Book 27

About the Author: Margaret Hepworth | The Gandhi Experiment

Author | Educator | Facilitator

Margaret Hepworth of The Gandhi Experiment

Margaret Hepworth is a thought leader in peace and values education and an expert in teenage motivations and behavior.

Founder of The Gandhi Experiment, whose vision is *world peace through education,* her drive and commitment for social justice has grown and flourished through her secondary teaching of 30 years. It has culminated in the highly successful conferences for students and adults: *Global Participation – it starts with us!*

Author of the forthcoming book: The Gandhi Experiment: Teaching our teenagers how to become global citizens (Rupa Publications, 2017), Margaret has completed a Master of Educational Studies (*Monash University, Australia*). The proud recipient of the 2016 *Sir John Monash Award for Inspirational Women's Leadership*, Margaret was also Head of Campus (Vice-Principal) at Preshil School (Melbourne, Australia).

Margaret's first novel, Clarity in Time, was published in 2012 (*Balboa Press*). The protagonist in the novel comes to understand that to make a difference in this world, you can no longer remain a passive by-stander.

A vibrant presenter, she is well versed in public speaking. Margaret has facilitated at international conferences, workshops and speaks at assemblies. Her interesting and varied background includes travelling widely. An Australian educator, she has also spent time living and teaching in the USA and Nanjing, China. Recent travels across India, Pakistan and Indonesia, where she facilitated teacher and student workshops in *Global Participation – it starts with us!* have broadened her outlook on peace education and life in general.

Above all, her belief in what she is trying to achieve (to help others step up to make a difference) gives Margaret the drive, passion and commitment to achieve peace in this world.

Margaret Hepworth

margaret@margarethepworth.com

www.thegandhiexperiment.com

Melbourne, Australia

Telephone: +61422154875

Margaret Hepworth is a passionate and committed educator. She is driven in her work by a strong social conscience which she draws on to encourage students to act in powerful and meaningful ways to leave their mark on the world and have a positive impact. Being a highly effective communicator she sweeps you up with her enthusiasm and inspires students and staff alike to consider the big questions of life.

- *Jonathan Walter, Principal Woodleigh School*

The Gandhi Experiment - the freshest ideas in mindful education!

Comments from participants in Collaborative Debating © workshops

'It will change the way I approach education.'

'A thought provoking topic'

'This has the potential to shift the way things are done'

'I feel 'inspired' 'enlightened' 'invigorated' 'grateful.'

'This gives us better ways to engage with conflict.'

'Instead of spiraling down into conflict and frustration, we in-spiraled up into cooperation and understanding.'

'In the beginning I didn't quite recognize what I was feeling as I debated; eventually it dawned on me – I was feeling calm.'

A request from the author

As founder and director of The Gandhi Experiment, I have a firm belief in equity in education. Alongside my paid work, I have worked countless voluntary hours, bringing values education into schools. This has been achieved through the *Global Participation – it starts with us!* student program, teacher training and *The Thriving Teens / Thriving Parents* parent seminars. In order to sustain this work, and to allow creativity for more educational products to be published, please purchase the number of manuals required for your school / organization – don't stop at one!

Read the sections in the manual on *Change begins with me* and *Stilled Silence* carefully. Find that inner governance. If we are going to make a difference in this world, it really does begin with a subtle, transformational shift within ourselves.

"Out beyond ideas of rightdoing and wrongdoing there is a field. I will meet you there."

- Rumi, 13th century Sufi poet

Why Collaborative Debating?

Ask yourself these questions: If we are successfully teaching certain values (e.g. collaboration, cooperation, sharing, kindness, respect, valuing others' opinions, empathy, compassion and so on), then why does it appear that these values are not being successfully transferred into the workplace, the global community, and politics? Why are there still such confronting issues in our world - racial discrimination, domestic violence, war, poverty, inequity in education, corruption? We have evolved physically. Why haven't we also evolved socially and emotionally? Why haven't we evolved to a point where we can live more harmoniously, in our diversity, across our planet?

Perhaps we talk too much about the need for change, yet don't address <u>how</u> we can <u>learn</u> to change.

Recently, I paused in my lengthy teaching career to ask myself these very same questions. I stepped out of the busyness of school life, to see if I could *reach in* to find some answers. I discovered areas we were teaching that appeared to be in open conflict with the values we hoped to instill. One such area that we teach students (perhaps without even realising the long term impact and societal implications), is to be adversarial when it comes to putting forward our arguments to *win* a debate.

I recall a time many years ago, as a student, myself, in the school debating team. I swooped on my *opponent* and floored her with my academic prowess. I was rewarded with extra points for my quick wittedness to find the hole in her argument, then undo her seamlessly. I felt great, a winner. She felt vulnerable and rejected, a loser.

As teachers, we need to look outward, to the society that our students will rapidly become a part of. Don't you wish to equip them with the skills that will enhance our growth as a community? To be constructive; to build a cohesive and inclusive society? With the issues our young people will face as they move forward, let us prepare them, beyond the classroom. Prepare them to navigate relationships towards fruitful and sustainable outcomes.

It is time to learn a new framework: one that recognises the need to hone our skills. Skills such as conflict negotiation, positing an argument, in expressing thought and opinion. Yet, this time, through respect and collaboration.

> *"It's not about changing minds*
> *– it's about opening new mind space."*
>
> *- Adult participant in a Collaborative Debate*

Educational Theory and Practices Underpinning Collaborative Debating

- ✓ Critical thinking: Teach a meta-cognitive approach: thinking about our thinking. Learning about our learning. To understand that we are constructs of our time, place and culture. Let's understand how texts position us to think and respond in a particular way. Let's get brave enough to allow our teenagers to challenge us! Let's hold courageous conversations!

- ✓ Utilising the power of creative energy in a classroom. Enjoy teaching teenagers and be in-joy with these young people. Working with their energetic flow, not against it.

- ✓ If we are going to make real change, we need to demonstrate a different way of thinking. Here we are employing Einstein's mantra: "We cannot solve our problems with the same thinking that we used to create them." For example, instead of "We own the planet" (a paradigm often embedded in the psyche of large corporations, and hence, resulting in destructive behaviours), we need to shift to "We are custodians of the planet." In fact, the latter has existed for millennia within our tribal nations across the planet. Think about the shift in a worldly perspective when we move from *I win, you lose*, to *when I win, you win too.* We must find new activities and educational tools to teach this paradigm to our young people.

- ✓ Positive thinking: *Flood their minds with hope*. Positive Psychology has shed *new light* on something I have always observed in working with teenagers. When faced with overwhelm, layers and layers of negativity (too much of the *bad stuff* that is happening out there), young people are more inclined to throw up their hands. They *give in* and move to a point of despair and apathy. Contrast this to what happens when teenagers are also taught about the *good stuff* - people finding solutions and taking action for positive change. Our young people then move to a point of action and positive engagement themselves. Hope stimulates action; action spurs hope. Do not mistake this with the idea that we won't be addressing the very real problems in our world. We address both problems *out there globally* and *very close to home*. We meet these issues head on through our Courageous Conversations. Yet, instead of simply learning that there is a problem, we manifest positivity by

learning about solutions. This concept is explored further in 'The Utopian Scale', a chapter in <u>The Gandhi Experiment – teaching our teenagers how to become global citizens</u>. Collaborative Debating is a solution focused view on addressing issues impacting us.
- ✓ Parallel thinking: based on Edward de Bono's concept of Parallel Thinking. This posits the idea that we don't all need to tread the same pathway to find the solution to a problem, or to reach the end goal. I can do it *my way*, you can do it *your way* and we can be supportive of *each other's way*.

Two Important Methodologies
The Still, Small Voice Within

Gandhi spoke of the still, small voice within - his voice of inner guidance or inner governance. He said, "The only tyrant I accept in this world is the still, small voice within me."

This is the voice he accessed through quiet times of meditation and prayer. It is this voice that gave him insight into his own behaviour towards others. It allowed wisdoms and insights to come to him. And gave him a deep sense of clarity in his next step forward, to action his truths. Fortunately for all of us, the *still, small voice* isn't a privilege or skill held only by Gandhi. It is in all of us. However, many of us haven't realised or learnt to access it yet. One of the most transformational things we can do in education is to teach our young people to actively practice accessing that voice of inner guidance.

We begin this process in Collaborative Debating, during the times of silence called for by the Mentor (formerly the adjudicator) in mid blustery debate; Stilled Silence. This takes place during the debate, particularly if arguments become heated in any way. Calling a moment of silence will pull everyone in the room back to a place of being centered; of being open minded, respectful and awake to their own truths and rationality.

Stilled Silence can do even more. Prior to the conclusion of the debate, the Mentor will call again for Stilled Silence. This is now a request to listen to wisdoms and fresh insights that might come *floating in*. New perspectives, new thoughts, a way of joining the dots of various people's arguments. New questions may arise. These are the questions we would now need to pursue if we are really going to get closer to actionable answers.

If our young people learn *Stilled Silence* as a skill to use in any aspect of their lives - in arguments with friends, conflict at home, tension in a workplace - can you imagine what this would mean for their futures?

Teacher's Note:

The use of stilled silence is invaluable. The earlier our young people learn

> this, the better for themselves and all around them. Read the chapter 'The Conundrum of Inner Listening', in my book <u>The Gandhi Experiment – Teaching our teenagers how to become global citizens.</u> It contains a number of activities for young people to learn to access their inner voice of guidance. (See details at the end of this manual, on how to purchase the book).

Change Begins With Me!

It has become somewhat of a cliché in our culture, yet *Change begins with me* has deep meaning and even deeper application. When you see something that you believe requires changing, that *thing* you observe (that appears to sit outside of you), well, that change actually begins with you. That is the essence of what *Change begins with me* is all about.

Interestingly, it is a common misconception that Gandhi said, "Be the change you wish to see in this world." What he did say, and I paraphrase somewhat, is that if you can change yourself within, then the world around you will change. We often question what our politicians are doing or the woes of the world - global concerns. Instead of constantly questioning *what needs to happen* externally, why not examine the change that can begin within?

One small, yet poignant example: As a teacher, observe what happens if you change <u>your</u> behaviour in the classroom. Notice its ripple effect on your students.

Personally, I like the fact that someone created a clever, catchy phrase: "Be the change you wish to see in this world." For me, the emphasis is on the *Be*. Once I have found the change I wish to be, then: *Be it, do it, act it – now!*

In Collaborative Debating, *Change begins with me* may mean a number of things:

- I will be prepared to change my point of view midway through a debate.
- I may learn to say "I'm sorry;" to admit "I didn't know that."
- I will learn to enter the debate with an attitude of respect for others.
- I will come prepared to actively listen to the other team.

- I believe that differences of opinion can sometimes lead to a magical outcome because they raise points / obstacles that I had not thought of before.

If change really does begin with me, then, as teachers, let's change the way we approach debate. In doing so, let us reflect upon the deeper implications this has for building a more cohesive society. We acknowledge that anger and conflict are natural and normal. Differences of opinion will always take place; emotions will run high. Yet we can teach better ways to handle conflict. To seek outcomes rather than stay stuck, embedded in emotion; to make our emotions constructively useful. The best place to begin? To change within.

Share these thoughts with your students:

Ask them: What does 'Change begins with me' mean? What are three things they could do, right now, to begin to *be the change they wish to see in this world?*

Yet, be forewarned: the deeper you enter into the concept of Change begins with me, the more challenged you will become - in the most thought provoking and enlightening way!

Key Learnings and Outcomes of Collaborative Debating

- ✓ The *win* is the solution to the problem, not a win over another person or team.
- ✓ We don't need to be judged, ranked or scored to learn, to strive, to thrive.
- ✓ It will be understood that there are multiple solutions to a problem.
- ✓ The element of rebuttal turns to looking for the positives and *additions* in another's argument.
- ✓ Respect can be learnt and celebrated.
- ✓ The development of active listening skills.
- ✓ It may be seen that we need to change the question or the proposition, before we can find a solution.
- ✓ Higher order thinking skills: such as analysing, evaluating, creating, and problem solving.
- ✓ That change really does begin with me.
- ✓ Learning what it actually means to work collaboratively.
- ✓ Change the dominant paradigm of *I win you lose*, to *when I win, you win too*.

Your students will meet the General Capabilities of:

- ✓ Critical and creative thinking
- ✓ Ethical understanding
- ✓ Personal and social capability

Students will develop their language and literacy skills, including:

- ✓ Knowledge, understanding and skills in listening, reading, viewing, speaking, writing and creating.
- ✓ Communication skills: listening, viewing.
- ✓ Analysing, developing, justifying and evaluating.
- ✓ Expressing and developing ideas.
- ✓ Formulate and articulate complex arguments.
- ✓ Public speaking.
- ✓ Understand context.
- ✓ Confidence building.

- ✓ To be a *successful learner, confident and creative individual, and active and informed citizen* (Australian Curriculum): whilst learning how to successfully collaborate with others.

Collaborative Debating Begins

In schools, Collaborative Debates are usually structured in the same form as a traditional school debate. That is, in two teams of three speakers. The very same skills can, however, also be applied to other situations e.g. a staff meeting, a student forum, at home in a family discussion, or even in a board room. To find out more about all these applications, please contact The Gandhi Experiment: www.thegandhiexperiment.com My ideal would be to see Collaborative Debating taught in the grand houses of Parliament!

Let's Set Up a Collaborative Debate in a Classroom

Two teams of three people are formed, with each speaker given a set time to speak. This is usually between 3-5 minutes, depending on the age and experience of your speakers.

However, from here, the debate takes a decidedly liberal and hearty turn from the adversarial debate of yore.

Titles

The first team is known as the **Affirmative** team.

The second team is now called the **Cooperative** team.

Instead of a Chairperson, we now have an **MC** - a **Mindful Coordinator**.

Instead of an Adjudicator - we have a **Mentor**.

Unfortunately, we still need a **Time keeper** (although we would love to have all the time in the world to solve the problem at hand)!

Language

Look at the way language shapes and re-frames everything:

The two teams now both have positive names: the Affirmative team remains the same, and instead of the traditional Negative team, we now have the Cooperative team. Think about how this positions the speakers. Whilst they still come to the debate from opposing views on the topic, thereby presenting differing opinions, they also enter the debate from the standpoint of being there to cooperate. They may be on opposing teams, yet they are not oppositional in attitude.

Instead of a Chairperson, rigidly holding to rules, the <u>Mindful Coordinator</u> brings a mindful presence into the room, whilst coordinating the flow of speakers.

Simply by renaming the <u>Adjudicator</u> as the Mentor, we remove the connotations of *judgment*, *presiding over* and *dispute*.

> *Discuss the use of language with your class:*
>
> The language we choose to use alters the nature of the space in which the Collaborative Debate is about to take place.
>
> "Why are we changing the framework of a traditional debate? Why are we using different names for the debating roles?"
>
> In the first few debates with your students, use critical thinking and meta-cognition. Discuss the changes that occur in our minds simply by altering the labels: Cooperative team, Mindful Coordinator and Mentor.

Space

Two teams of three sit on opposite sides of the front of the room, at desks or tables.

The Mindful Coordinator and Timekeeper sit between the two teams.

The rest of the class makes up the audience.

The Mentor is best placed central, towards the back of the room, yet where everyone can see and hear her/him. The Mentor is the pivotal role in the debate, as you will see. The Mentor is a reminder, a symbol and guardian of respect. It is through the Mentor's Guidances that clarity will emerge through the debate.

We are mindful, not just of the physical positions of those participating in the debate, but also to the space we are creating – a trusted space. The Mentor reminds everyone: "In the centre of the room and radiating out to all corners of the room, sits *respect*."

Celebration

By the end of the debate, we are celebrating a collective win - finding a solution to the problem.

Collaborative Debating - The Process

1. The Mentor begins by framing the debate:

Mentor: "There will be no judging, no scores, no grading or degrading. Instead, there will be guidance, suggestions, and acceptance of suggestions in return.

"Human beings are naturally competitive. But what we are seeking is healthy competition, healthy debate. Not over-competition to the point of greed, *I win at all costs*.

"So, the Affirmative team is striving to speak for the proposition.

"The Cooperative team is striving to speak against the proposition.

"However, each team is prepared to: listen, take on board the other team's points, make suggestions, and build on the movement towards an answer to the problem.

"Instead of seeking to be adversarial, we are seeking to be cooperative. Instead of framing or positioning ourselves in defiant opposition, we are positioning ourselves as collaborators.

"We want to find a solution to the problem or proposition."

2. Planning and setting roles:

a. Once the topic has been set (see suggested topics below), allow planning time. The time given to planning and debate preparation is up to you as the teacher. For example, some debates are given very little planning time – i.e. half an hour. Others are set for homework - one week ahead of the debate.

b. Set the time allowance for speakers - e.g. 3 minutes or 5 minutes for each speaker. The Time keeper will ring a bell once 30 seconds before time, and give two rings when the speaker has reached their time allocation. The time allowance given depends on the age and experience of the debaters.

3. The role of the Mindful Coordinator is to introduce each speaker to stand and speak in turn. Beginning with the first speaker for the Affirmative team and alternating through each team, first speaker for the Cooperative team etc., until all speakers have spoken. If necessary, the Mindful Coordinator will also remind people of the need for respect. Once they become proficient at their role, they may even aid the Mentor with the Guidances (see below). They may make suggestions during the debate, which will add to the fullness of the ensuing discussion. The Mindful Coordinator may also note down new issues and poignant questions that are raised as the debate progresses.

4. The Mentor will use a series of Guidances, as set out below. These are to be implemented at the conclusion of each speech. As the Mentor sits through more debates, they will become more proficient at knowing which Guidance to use and when to use them. They may even add their own. Please note: Speakers are not interrupted by the Mentor; Guidances are given respectfully when a speaker has finished speaking.

However, there is an exception to every rule. I have, *at rare times*, found it very useful to pause a speaker, mid-speech, to remind them of their commitment to a previous guidance. This is outlined in the example below. As noted, this is rarely the case.

Both students and teachers can be trained in the role of Mentor. It is initially the role of a teacher. It is useful to have the list of Guidances next to the Mentor, for easy reference during the debate.

5. Instead of rebuttal, we now have additions. That is, we are seeking to build on the debate rather than howl someone's argument down. Examples of this might include a speaker stating: "We agree with what you said about _____. However, you might like to consider…" Or "That's a really interesting point you made about _____, yet we are not sure of its validity. Perhaps you could do more research in _____." Or "We really like what you said about _____. We believe this very same idea could be used to expand _____." Language and tone frame our attitudes and our willingness to participate in a collaborative effort.

> *Introducing the concept of Additions needs to occur prior to the debate:*
>
> Learning how to Add rather than Detract:
>
> Practice with your class how you might add to someone's argument,

> rather than detract from it; or creatively build towards a solution – even if you disagree with their viewpoint.
>
> "How can you present a strong argument for your case and yet be open to actively listening to the other team's opinions?'
>
> "If you still disagree with them after listening to them, how will you make them aware of this, respectfully? Constructively?"

Topics, propositions and provocations:

You may choose to simply hand out topics, always framed as a proposition: "We are having debates next week. Here are the Propositions… Let's work out the teams…"

Or, you may like to think of a creative way to introduce the debating topic/proposition itself. Here is just one example, in the form of a provocation. As research tells us, humans become far more engaged, and ready to really take something on, when they *feel passionate* about it. They become *moved to do* something about the situation. This gives the debate an air of realism, rather than simply an academic exercise to argue about something. Some students may choose to actively pursue these topics as projects after the debate.

> *Example of a Provocation:*
>
> Ask your class: "Did anyone hear on the news this morning that the government has announced that Australia (or insert your country here) is introducing a Two-child Policy in two years' time?"
>
> Invite opinions: "What do you think of the idea that our government would be instituting a policy that stipulates how many children you can have i.e. two?" (Please note: You haven't actually told a lie and said this is happening. You have simply asked "Did anyone hear this in the news this morning?")
>
> "How might this impact you personally?
>
> "How might it impact our country?
>
> "Which is the only country in the world that has ever enforced a one-child policy (the answer, of course, is China)? Why would China have done this? What effect has it had on their country?"

> Allow your students to explore their immediate reactions to the concept of a two-child policy in their country: thoughts, feelings, reactions. Then, reveal to them, the reality. "Did anyone hear on the news this morning that the government has announced that Australia (or your country) will be introducing a two-child policy in two years time? Well, no, of course you didn't because it isn't real or true. Why might I have framed the debate in this way? (Meta-cognition.) We are, however, going to hold a debate about this very topic.
>
> "The proposition for our debate is:
>
> *"That Australia (or your country) should introduce a two-child policy."*
>
> The collaborative debate can then be organized as such: two teams of three, alternating speakers from each team. The Affirmative team speaks in support of the proposition; the Cooperative team speaks against the proposition.

You can, if preferred, have a less formal structure and hold a full class debate / forum, with everyone having the right to speak. The same Mentor Guidelines would be utilised. This alternative structure will be explored further at The Gandhi Experiment website www.thegandhiexperiment.com.

Remember, we are still looking for a persuasive speech. Quality and clarity of the argument's content, appeal to the facts and experts, emotional stories, team line etc. But we are not judging, scoring, nor awarding points. We are listening, creating and responding; acknowledging that there is a problem, and building a solution together.

The Mentor's Guidances

It is the role of the Mentor to stop the debate at the end of each speech, and *make a call* - a *Guidance*. This allows everyone in the room to monitor the flow of argument. It provides time to think and reconsider positions and maintain respectful debate.

The Mentor's Guidances include, but are not excluded, to:

1. "On this point alone, I stand with you." This call from the Mentor takes place at the conclusion of a debater's speech. This call can take place many times throughout the debate, and helps clarify the path the debate is taking. For example: At the conclusion of the first speaker for the Affirmative's speech, the Mentor addresses the Cooperative team. "The first speaker has said that the world is overpopulated. On this point alone, do you stand with her?" Those members of the Cooperative team, who agree with that point, now stand to show they concur. They then sit. It is best, early in the debate, to do this just with the speakers of the two debating teams. You may choose to invite the speaker to explain this point further (or simply leave it at that). There are members of the other team who agree with that point being made, even if they do not agree with the entire speech. As the debate progresses, invite all members of the audience to respond. For example: "The second speaker for the Cooperative team has said, 'No government has the right to dictate how many children a couple can choose to have.' On this point alone, do you stand with the speaker?" You may like to ask one or two members of the audience why they are standing for this point. Ask one or two members of the audience why they have chosen to remain seated.

2. "Is anyone prepared to reconsider their own proposition?" This guidance would be asked three-quarters of the way through the debate.

3. "Does anyone want to disagree with a particular point?" Ask the teams. Ask the audience.

4. "Is anyone feeling conflicted within themselves right now? Can you try to explain why?" This guidance allows for a *conscience vote.*

5. "You may now cross the floor, if you wish." Speakers are free to move to the other team, to show they have changed their mind on a particular point (or on the debate as a whole). It is interesting to ask how someone became persuaded to *change sides*. What was it exactly that influenced them to re-think their position? Once people have crossed the floor to show where they now stand, they then return to their team and the debate continues.

6. Audience involvement: Choose strategic times to invite the audience to respond, by standing to some of the Guidances above.

7. Stilled Silence: "We are going to stop the debate for one minute to listen to our inner voice." After one minute: "Does anyone have new insights to shed on the debate thus far?" The Mentor can call this guidance at any time.

8. A final Stilled Silence - to see what else comes up on this particular topic. "We have heard all speakers and from some members of the audience as well. Let's have a final minute (or two) of Stilled Silence, to see what other wisdoms and insights may come to us. And how these might help us find a solution to the problems we have raised through the debate."

9. "Move to show where you stand." This can be used as the final guidance, to indicate where the feelings and thoughts of the debaters now lie at the conclusion of the debate. Debaters literally move to the team they now most agree with. The audience can also be asked to move, to show where they stand.

10. Have we resolved the problem? Is there, perhaps, a more appropriate proposition or topic? Do we need to hold another debate with a refined topic, so we get closer to a real solution?

> *Remember to find other times, well outside the debate, to practice Stilled Silence – inner listening. This skill will aid our young people in all aspects of life. Read the chapter 'The Conundrum of Inner Listening', in* The Gandhi Experiment book: Teaching our teenagers how to become global citizens *by Margaret Hepworth.*

Teacher's Note: You can find further explanation of the Mentor Guidances at www.thegandhiexperiment.com by keying in to our newsletter. You can also book a Collaborative Debating workshop through the website.

Learning to Give the Mentor Guidances

When you begin practice Collaborative Debates with your students, for a while there, <u>you</u> will be <u>practicing</u> the role of the Mentor. You may feel you are also learning new skills, or this may be something you already feel very accomplished at. Whenever you learn something new, the way forward is to keep giving it a go, until you feel confident about it.

Key points to focus on as the Mentor:

- ✓ Stay present in the debate. Don't allow other thoughts to distract you.
- ✓ Employ active listening skills to *pull out* the key points of the debate – to call the Guidance: *On this point, I stand with you*.
- ✓ Keep the list of Guidances next to you, selecting the most useful ones at particular points in the debate.
- ✓ Listen for contradictions in the students' speeches. Then, call for agreement or disagreement.
- ✓ Challenge extreme points: *Stand up if you agree that _____*. We are challenging in a measured and respectful way, not degrading anyone. I have seen it happen with extreme arguments (i.e. arguing for the sake of arguing) that nobody stands to agree – not even the speaker who has made the *grand claim*! It becomes clear to them, then, that they are only arguing for other reasons - to win the point, to find a loop hole, to appear to be clever. They are not supporting the premise of Collaborative Debating – to find a solution to the problem.
- ✓ Find time to practice Stilled Silence with your students; find time to practice it yourself. This will assist everyone in understanding the power of *stilling* the debate for one minute. And to understand that this can clear the way for new insights.

"I found the role of the Mentor gave space to reflect on key points / highlighted areas of agreement which contributed significantly to collaborative engagement of both teams."

"I loved the Mentor's role of closely listening to each speaker, noting their points and checking/clarifying with listeners. This helped to process each person's points before rushing to the next as so often happens.

Collaborative Debating participants

One Example of a Mentor's Guidance Where a Speaker was Interrupted

During a Collaborative Debate (held at a well known boys' school in Melbourne), early on I called the following Guidance. Please note: this was the first time they had been introduced to Collaborative Debating. As a school well known for their traditional debating prowess, many were still setting out to "win at all costs."

My Guidance: "On this point alone, I stand with you: The first speaker for the Affirmative team has said, 'We believe that every person is entitled to a happy and healthy standard of living. On this point alone, who in the room stands with him?" Every person in the room stood in agreement with this.

So, when the first speaker for the Cooperative team began a line of thought that ran contrary to this, as the Mentor, I was able to stop the whole debate, mid speech. I asked, "You just agreed that every person had the right to a happy and healthy lifestyle. Yet now you are suggesting something else entirely - leaving babies out for the wolves."

This team had thought they would be very clever and win the debate by arguing a loop-hole: that we should not have a two child policy, we should have a zero child policy. They had still held to the idea that you needed to win the debate, not solve the problem. By stopping the debate, I got them to recognise they had agreed to this point of well-being for all. They then needed to proceed with a different line of argument. It was not worth arguing, simply for the sake of being the victor in an argument.

At the conclusion of this debate, every person on the Cooperative team crossed the floor, to join the Affirmative team. Afterwards, the most logical, sequential, highly competitive, traditional adversarial debater approached me. He looked directly at me, smiled a beaming smile and said, "I like your Collaborative Debating." I left feeling positively affirmed. If, in the space of one Collaborative Debate, that young man could see the benefits - that was hope for our future.

Teaching the Role of Mentor to your Students
Case Study: Templestowe College

As we were setting up the debate - presenting the proposition, forming the teams, selecting a Mindful Coordinator and Timekeeper and agreeing how long preparation time would be, one student, Simon, raised his hand, "Can I sit next to you and learn how to be the Mentor?"

Brilliant, I thought. Not just the fact that, right from the start, I would have a Mentor-in-training. But, perhaps more importantly, I was acknowledging this young man's attitude. He was keen, open to the concept of Mentoring and ready to learn. "Absolutely! Yes," I replied. To be honest, I wasn't sure how he would go. The whole class was learning this completely new framework for debating – well, a new way of thinking.

Next lesson: In preparation for our first Collaborative Debate, the students re-arranged the classroom. Simon moved his seat next to mine. We sat towards the back of the classroom, to scan the two teams and audience.

The debate began.

By the time the second speaker for the Affirmative had spoken, Simon was selecting his own "On this point alone" Guidances. He was writing them down and pushing them over to me to consider. "Ask it," I prompted. Simon stood: "Elonie said_____. On this point alone, can the members of the Cooperative team please stand, if you agree with this statement?" One team member stood. "Can you please explain why you agree?" His experience of being a Mentor had begun!

By the conclusion of this one debate, Simon had learnt to confidently handle several Guidances. This was purely by observing me modelling the process. Sometimes I would point at the Guidance list, to a call I had previously made. "Would anyone like to cross the floor to stand next to someone they have been persuaded by?" "Can we have one minute of Stilled Silence to reflect on what has just been said?"

I believe the best way to teach a student the Mentor role is to do precisely this – to model it. To model it successfully, you need to become proficient at it yourself. So, run a few Collaborative Debates with yourself as the Mentor first. Then you could introduce a Mentor-in-training. However, remember this: with every Collaborative Debate, you are modelling Mentor Guidances, i.e. skills for unravelling conflict, to every member of your classroom / audience. They will then use these skills in their own lives, beyond the classroom. This afterall, is our aim.

Suggested Topics for Debates

Topics for debates are endless. Here are just a few suggestions. Please remember, debate topics are framed as propositions. The proposition is not expressing the opinion of the teacher, or person putting it forward. It is simply framed in a particular way, to encourage debate.

That our government needs to rethink its asylum seeker policy.

That we should only sell fair-trade chocolate in the canteen.

That we should do away with a school uniform.

That all schools should be co-educational schools.

That euthanasia should be a legal choice.

That homework should be banned.

That capitalism is better than socialism.

That religion does more harm than good.

That the United Nations has failed in its purpose.

That everyone in the world should become vegetarian.

Conclusion

When you are ready, draw a deep breath and read back over the entire manual. This time, as you read, imagine you are a future politician entering the halls of Parliament. Having studied Collaborative Debating, you ask yourself: In what ways can I cooperate with the other political parties? In what ways can I find the best outcomes and solutions for our country?

Now, as a teacher, remind yourself just who it is that we are teaching, and what they will become.

Again, I reiterate, if our young people learn to use this tool in every aspect of their lives - in arguments with friends, conflict at home, tension in a workplace - can you imagine what this would mean for their futures?

*"Yesterday I was clever, so I wanted to change the world.
Today I am wise, so I am changing myself."*

- *Rumi*

Other Uses of the Collaborative Debating Technique

Interested in learning more about Collaborative Debating

- In the school context: as a student forum; class debate; or staff meeting?
- In the home: a family discussion; resolving a family dispute?

Or:

- How this technique can transform a boardroom or political arena?

Then please contact The Gandhi Experiment, Margaret@margarethepworth.com to access our packages available online soon.

Through our newsletter and website: You will discover video clips to help you with Mentor Guidances and assistance with creating interesting provocations.

Collaborative Debating is an Educational Tool for Social Change

Let's create a team effort, to re-shape the way we approach debate!

As life is a collaboration and we are all products of teamwork, please share your experiences with us, at The Gandhi Experiment, so we can place them on our website or Facebook page to share with others.

www.thegandhiexperiment.com

https://www.facebook.com/TheGandhiExperiment/

Examples of your posts to us could include: student comments, learnings, new Guidances created by your Mentors, your own observations, suggestions for improvement and more.

Let's create a win-win situation, where the solutions are carried beyond the classroom, into the 'real world' - the school yard, the staff workplace, the boardroom and our parliaments.

Contact us to organise a Collaborative Debating workshop in your school today!

COMING SOON: The NEW Gandhi Experiment Book
Teaching Our Teenagers How to Become Global Citizens
By Margaret Hepworth

Sign up at www.thegandhiexperiment.com to receive notification of this forthcoming publication in early 2017! This book includes more engaging activities for your classrooms:

- ✓ The Dinner Party to Save the World
- ✓ The Best Forgiveness Role Play Ever
- ✓ Einstein's Theory of Why? Why? Why?
- ✓ The Conundrum of Inner Listening
- ✓ The Utopian Scale
- ✓ 'Almost Impossible Thoughts'
- ✓ And more…

Also Coming Soon: A Brand New Activity: Come to My Table

Come to My Table helps people understand how to prepare for a potentially tense discussion. Not just *what* they want to say, but *how* to say it; to provide the best chance of an agreeable outcome for both sides.

Visit http://www.thegandhiexperiment.com for further details.

The Collaborative Debating methodology explores the beliefs which underpin our viewpoints in a collaborative, non-threatening manner. It allows for an exploration of commonality and middle-ground in our differences, thus providing a greater understanding of ourselves and others. I believe this can only ever be a good thing.

- *Sue Anderson, Founder, SKA Enterprises, skaenterprises.com.au*

Cutting edge education isn't about the use of technology; it is about creating a new framework to enable change.

- *Margaret Hepworth, 2016*

www.ingramcontent.com/pod-product-compliance
Lightning Source LLC
Chambersburg PA
CBHW042302010526
44113CB00047B/2770